Follow Me Around™
Greece

By Anna T. Tabachnik

SCHOLASTIC

Content Consultant: Elektra Kostopoulou, PhD
Instructor, Modern Greek Studies, Rutgers University, New Brunswick, New Jersey

Library of Congress Cataloging-in-Publication Data
Names: Tabachnik, Anna T., author.
Title: Greece / by Anna T. Tabachnik.
Description: New York, NY : Children's Press, 2019. | Series: Follow me around | Includes bibliographical references and index.
Identifiers: LCCN 2018009071 | ISBN 9780531129241 (library binding) | ISBN 9780531138663 (pbk.)
Subjects: LCSH: Greece—Juvenile literature.
Classification: LCC DF717 .T33 2019 | DDC 949.5—dc23
LC record available at https://lccn.loc.gov/2018009071

Design: Anna Tunick Tabatchnick
Creative Direction: Judith E. Christ for Scholastic Inc.
Text: Wiley Blevins
© 2019 Scholastic Inc.

All rights reserved. Published in 2019 by Children's Press, an imprint of Scholastic Inc.
Printed in North Mankato, MN, USA 113
SCHOLASTIC, CHILDREN'S PRESS, and associated logos are trademarks and/or registered trademarks of Scholastic Inc.
Scholastic Inc., 557 Broadway, New York, NY 10012

1 2 3 4 5 6 7 8 9 10 R 28 27 26 25 24 23 22 21 20 19

Photos ©: cover background: Andrew Mayovskyy/Shutterstock; cover children: Anthony Lee/age fotostock; back cover: Anthony Lee/age fotostock; 1: Anthony Lee/age fotostock; 3: MatiasEnElMundo/Getty Images; 4 left: Anthony Lee/age fotostock; 6: Morsa Images/Getty Images; 7 top left: Gatsi/iStockphoto; 7 bottom right: Thanasis Zovoilis/Getty Images; 8 top right: tolisma/iStockphoto; 8 center right top: bonchan/Shutterstock; 8 center bottom right: Joshua Resnic/Shutterstock; 8 bottom right: PhotonStock/iStockphoto; 8 left: Olive Images/Media Bakery; 9 top: robynmac/iStockphoto; 9 center: ac_bnphotos/iStockphoto; 9 bottom: Marccophoto/iStockphoto; 10: robertharding/Alamy Images; 11: Claudia Holzförster/Alamy Images; 12-13 god icons: MatiasEnElMundo/Getty Images; 12-13 background: Vadim Yerofeyev/Dreamstime; 13 bottom right: nld/Shutterstock; 14 top left: Christopher Furlong/Getty Images; 14 top right: Glenn van der Knijff/Getty Images; 14 bottom: Melanie Stetson Freeman/The Christian Science Monitor/Getty Images; 15 left: milosk50/Shutterstock; 15 right: George Tsafos/Getty Images; 16 left: Walter Bibikow/Getty Images; 16 center: Hemis/AWL Images; 16 right: Christophe Boisvieux/Getty Images; 17 left: Anna Fevraleva/Shutterstock; 17 right: Vladimir_Timofeev/iStockphoto; 18 left: Men vote to ostacise a fellow citizen in the Athenian Agora (colour litho), Herget, Herbert M. (1885-1950)/National Geographic Creative/Bridgeman Images; 18 center: Epaminondas defending Pelopidas, illustration from 'Plutarch's Lives for Boys and Girls', retold by W.H. Weston, London c.1910 (colour litho), Rainey, William (1852-1936)/Private Collection/The Stapleton Collection/Bridgeman Images; 18 right: DEA/M. CARRIERI/De Agostini/Getty Images; 19 left: A Greek Priest, 1844, Scherer, Joseph (1814-91)/Private Collection/Photo © Christie's Images/Bridgeman Images; 19 center: De Agostini Picture Library/Getty Images; 19 right: Marian Weyo/Shutterstock; 20 left: imagedj/Shutterstock; 20 right: DEA/G. DAGLI ORTI/Getty Images; 21 right: British Library/akg-images/The Image Works; 21 left: Alessandro0770/Dreamstime; 22: SAKIS MITROLIDIS/AFP/Getty Images; 23 right: Terry Harris/Alamy Images; 23 top left: Andrey_Popov/Shutterstock; 23 center left top: Dimitrios Manis/SOPA Images/LightRocket/Getty Images; 23 center left bottom: ZUMA Press, Inc./Newscom; 23 bottom left: Nikolas Georgiou/ZUMA Press, Inc./Alamy Images; 24 left: Odyssey-Images/Alamy Images; 24 center right: In earliest times a simple foot-race was the only event, illustration from The Story of Greece by Mary Macgregor, 1st edition, 1913 (colour print), Crane, Walter (1845-1915)/Private Collection/The Stapleton Collection/Bridgeman Images; 24 top right-25 left: Alexander Hassenstein/Bongarts/Getty Images; 25 right: TravelCollection/Alamy Images; 26 left: kefkenadasi/iStockphoto; 26 right: Dean Drobo/Shutterstock; 27 bottom: gerenme/iStockphoto; 27 top left: Photostella/Dreamstime; 28 A.: Danita Delimont/Alamy Images; 28 B.: Photobac/Shutterstock; 28 C.: George Tsafos/Getty Images; 28 D.: Hercules Milas/Alamy Images; 28 E.: Jochen Schlenker/age fotostock; 28 F.: Nataliya Nazarov/Shutterstock; 28 G: newsfocus1/iStockphoto; 30 top right: grebeshkovmaxim/Shutterstock; 30 top left: Leontura/Getty Images; 30 bottom: Anthony Lee/age fotostock.

Maps by Jim McMahon/Mapman ®.

9-2018

Front cover:
Santorini at sunset

2

Table of Contents

USA

GREECE

Where in the World Is Greece?

Yasu from Greece! That's how we say "hello." I'm Alexandra, and this is my twin brother, Yiorgos (YOR-gohs). Thousands of years ago, Greek lands were the center of a very important **civilization**. My own name, Alexandra, is about 3,000 years old! Many of Greece's inventions and ideas about politics, science, sports, and art are part of modern Western life today. Even our stories, called **myths**, about monsters, magical creatures, and the gods Greeks worshipped long ago are famous. Come on—let us show you around!

Fast Facts:

- Greece covers 50,949 square miles (131,957 square kilometers).

- Greece is in Europe on the Balkan **Peninsula**. To the north are Albania, the Republic of Macedonia, and Bulgaria. Turkey lies to the northeast. Italy is to the west.

- The Mediterranean Sea surrounds Greece's mainland on three sides.

- Greece has more than 2,000 islands that make up nearly 20 percent of the country's land. People live on only about 170 of them.

- Mountains cover 80 percent of Greece. The tallest, Mount Olympus, is 9,570 feet (2,917 meters) high. In our myths, it is the home of the ancient gods.

SERBIA

ROMANIA

MONTENEGRO

KOSOVO

BULGARIA

Black Sea

REPUBLIC OF MACEDONIA

ALBANIA

Thessaloniki

Sea of Marmara

TURKEY

Mount Olympus

CORFU

GREECE

Aegean Sea

Athens

Corinth

Sparta

RHODES

CRETE

Mediterranean Sea

N
W E
S

Home Sweet Home

We live in Athens. It is a busy city! Like many of our friends, we leave the city on weekends and holidays. We visit our *yia-yiá* (yah-YAH, grandmother) in her village. She is my father's mother. Family is very important in Greece. Older family members are treated with respect.

In many ways, families hold Greece together. Kids usually live with their parents until getting married in their late 20s or early 30s. In addition, many businesses are small and run by families. When people are sick or lose their job, they often turn to their families for help.

Freshly picked olives

Pride and Respect

Filotimo is a Greek word that can be translated as "to be proud." To us, it describes how we live our lives. Here are four ways we carry it out:

1. **Doing good deeds**, even (and especially) if no one will notice.

2. **Treating** our elders respectfully.

3. **Taking pride** in our family's and country's history and culture.

4. **Welcoming others** with generosity and hospitality.

About one out of five people in Greece live in the countryside. There are a lot of family farms! Everyone pitches in. Even small children can collect eggs from a henhouse or feed the sheep. Feta, a salty, crumbly cheese, is made with sheep's milk. Olives, mostly used to make oil, are the most common crop on family farms. They are also the most traditional. In fact, olives have been grown in Greece for more than 5,500 years!

Grandfather and grandson

Koulouri

Moussaka

Gyro

Baklava

Let's Eat!

In Greece, breakfast may be a *koulouri* (KOO-loo-ree), a bagel-like ring of bread covered in sesame seeds. A *tiropita* (tee-ROH-pee-tah), a cheese pastry, is also popular for breakfast. Of course, we might just have a bowl of cornflakes. For lunch, we sometimes have a spinach-cheese pie called *spanakopita* (spah-nah-KOH-pee-tah) or lentils. Our mom also makes *moussaka* (moo-sah-KAH). This dish has layers of eggplant, ground meat, and spices, with a creamy topping!

Seafood—from sea bass to shrimp—is a big part of our diet. Mussels, a relative of clams, are our father's favorite. People might also grab a *gyro* (YEE-roh) for lunch. It has slices of roasted pork inside pita bread. Onion, tomato, and a creamy yogurt-cucumber sauce called *tzatziki* (tsah-TSEE-kee) are added on top.

Dinner is a big event. Greeks eat late and linger with friends and family over large meals. We have small dishes to start. *Taramasalata* (tah-rah-mah-sah-LAH-tah) is a dip made from fish eggs. Another favorite is *dolmades* (dohl-MAH-dehs), grape leaves stuffed with herbs, rice, and sometimes meat. *Kolokithokeftedes* (koh-loh-kih-thah-kehf-TEH-dehs), fried zucchini balls, are also popular.

After that we might share a whole grilled fish with string beans and tomatoes topped with feta. *Domates yemistes* (doh-MAH-tehs yeh-MEES-tehs), tomatoes stuffed with rice and meat, may come with it.

We finish with dessert. My favorite is *baklava* (bah-klah-VAH), a crunchy pastry with crushed nuts that oozes with honey. Yum! Sometimes, we like to go for fast food, just like you.

All About Olives

Olives are stone fruits, just like plums and cherries. But don't try to eat an olive right off a tree. They're so bitter! Most olives you eat are soaked with lye and salt to remove the bitterness. There are dozens of kinds of Greek olives.

Kalamata

Our favorites are:
Kalamata—They are purple-black. They can't be eaten if they are picked green.

Amfissa

Amfissa—These are also dark in color. They are soft and have a mild taste.

Halkidiki

Halkidiki—This olive is only picked when green and has a bit of a pepper flavor.

In school, we study math, science, reading and writing, and many other subjects.

Off to School

Education is important in Greece. Everyone goes to school, which is free. School is competitive from a young age. Yiorgos and I like to see who can get closer to 20, the best grade. In Greece, young children often go to kindergarten, but we don't have to. The law says we must start school at age 6, in the first grade. Yiorgos and I are at a *dimotikó* (dee-moh-tee-KOH), elementary school. This year we're in fourth grade, which means we start music classes and a foreign language!

kaliteros filos
best friend

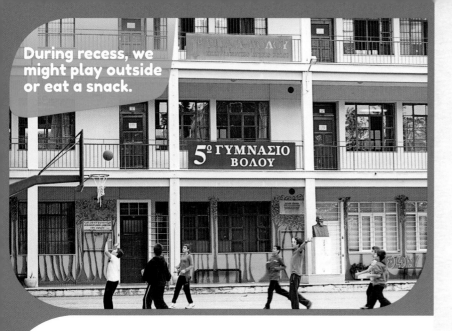

During recess, we might play outside or eat a snack.

5º ΓΥΜΝΑΣΙΟ ΒΟΛΟΥ

Our school day goes from 8 a.m. to 2 p.m. First thing in the morning, our class says a prayer together. Then we start our lessons. We have four 10- to 20-minute recesses, which happen between classes. We eat lunch at home after school. We also go to English school two evenings a week and have a math tutor who comes to our home.

We get the summers off from school, just like you. We also have four weeks of vacation during the school year: two weeks at Christmas and two at Easter.

If you visit Greece, it will be very useful to know a few numbers. Let's start with 1 through 10.

1 ένα (EH-nah)

2 δύο (THEE-oh)

3 τρία (TREE-ah)

4 τέσσερα (TEHS-ehr-ah)

5 πέντε (PEHN-deh)

6 έξι (EHK-see)

7 επτά (ehf-TAH)

8 οκτώ (ahk-TOH)

9 εννέα (eh-NAY-ah)

10 δέκα (THEHK-ah)

THE STORY OF
PERSEPHONE

In history class, we're studying old myths and folktales. The story of Persephone is my favorite one. It explains why we have seasons.

Demeter was the goddess who made the world's plants grow. Nobody wanted to upset her. If she was unhappy, crops would not thrive and people would starve. Demeter's greatest joy was her daughter, Persephone. As Persephone grew up, Hades, god of the dead and the underworld, fell in love with her. Demeter refused to let Hades marry her daughter.

Persephone

Demeter

Hades asked Zeus, king of the gods, for help. Zeus gave him permission to kidnap Persephone! One day, while Persephone was out picking flowers, the earth opened beneath her feet. Hades flew up in his chariot and snatched her. Demeter was desperate to find her daughter. As she searched, all the plants felt her sadness. The leaves turned brown and floated away in the wind. The figs rotted and fell. The

Hades

grass faded to straw. When Demeter learned what Hades had done, she was furious. She threatened Zeus that she would never let anything grow again unless Persephone was freed. Alarmed, Zeus sent his speedy messenger Hermes to rescue her.

Zeus

Hermes

Meanwhile, Hades worked to become friends with Persephone. He encouraged her to rule the underworld with him. He also brought her fruits and sweets.

At first, Persephone refused to eat. She knew if she ate food while there, she would be trapped forever. But she grew weak with hunger. And over time, she became fond of Hades. Persephone finally gave in and began to eat a ripe pomegranate. She had eaten six of the fruit's seeds when Hermes, the messenger, approached. Hermes knew he had to take Persephone home. He struck a deal with Hades. Persephone would spend six months of the year with him, one for each pomegranate seed she ate. She would spend the other six months on earth with her mother, Demeter.

Now each year, when Persephone descends to the underworld, Demeter mourns and autumn arrives. When Persephone returns to earth, Demeter's happiness brings the spring.

Pomegranate

Mural at a Metro station

National Garden

Touring Greece

Athens: Capital City

Athens is our home and the capital of Greece. It was named for Athena, the ancient Greek goddess of war and wisdom. Athens is a busy city with a speedy train system we call the Metro. The Metro is decorated with modern sculptures and colorful **murals**. Ancient Greek art and artifacts are also on display. I love to stop and look on my way through!

Evzones

Tourists and Athenians alike spend time in the National Garden. This public park is filled with greenery and flowering plants. It is just behind the parliament building, where our lawmakers meet. People who come on the hour can see the changing of the guard here. The guards, called *evzones*, protect our Tomb of the Unknown Soldier. They wear old-style uniforms of kilts and shoes with pom-poms.

Parthenon

Acropolis

Agora

People who want to explore ancient Athens can begin at the Acropolis. Athens began here about 2,500 years ago. This part of town is located high on a hill that overlooks the rest of the city. This is why it's sometimes called the "City at the Top." Ancient buildings stand here, including the Parthenon. This is a temple for the goddess Athena. There is also a museum that holds some of our most precious and ancient carvings and sculptures.

These pieces are white now. When they were first created, however, they were painted all over in bright colors.

Nearby is the Agora, the ancient city center. The public square was once a heart of activity. Ancient Athenians could shop, worship, vote, or just meet with their friends. You can still see the long, shaded walkways called colonnades. Today, people come to the neighborhood to visit the flea market and small shops, and see the stunning street art.

Vikos Gorge

Mount Athos

Mount Olympus

Mountains and Islands

There is more to Greece than the crowded streets of Athens. The country's mountains are beautiful. Zagorohoria in the north has tiny mountain villages and the world's deepest canyon, the Vikos Gorge. Our family once hiked through the gorge. On the mountain roads, look for roaming herds of goats. Drivers sometimes have to stop their cars and wait for them to move.

Farther east in Macedonia is the famous Mount Olympus. It is our tallest mountain. Our cousins love to trek all the way to the top of its 9,570-foot-high (2,917 m) peak. Sticking out into the Aegean Sea is another famous mountain: Mount Athos. This is an important place for the Greek Orthodox Church. Women are not allowed! Yiorgos and our dad visited it once. But our mom and I have only seen it from a distance.

Corfu

The palace at Knossos

Greece also has incredible islands. Corfu is one of them. Lemons and oranges, grapes and figs grow in its beautiful countryside. The island of Lefkada is known for its gorgeous beaches and clear blue waters.

My favorite island is Zakynthos. It has sea caves and a beach where loggerhead sea turtles lay their eggs every year. Yiorgos and I went **snorkeling** there. We saw a tortoise that was nearly as big as us!

The island of Crete has mountains and beaches. It is also home to ancient buildings such as the palace at Knossos. The palace was recently fixed up to make it look the way it might have when it was first built about 3,500 years ago. One famous myth tells the story of a Minotaur, who was half man and half bull. The Minotaur was kept prisoner at Knossos in a giant maze called a labyrinth.

Our Country's History

Greece has a long and interesting history. People have lived on this land for many thousands of years.

The first civilizations here were some of the oldest in Europe! Between 1000 BCE and 800 BCE, powerful cities, called *poleis*, began to grow. Among them were Sparta and Athens. These poleis developed cultures, religions, and governments. The poleis traded goods, fought, and made deals with one another and with other countries, including Persia and Egypt.

Timeline: Key Moments in Greek History

Athens

Sparta wins

Alexander the Great

507 BCE
Democracy Develops
Greece's first democracy begins in Athens. *Democracy* means "ruled by the people." However, only men over age 20 can vote.

431–404 BCE
Peloponnesian War
The Greek poleis of Athens and Sparta fight. Sparta wins with the help of nearby Persia, and the Spartans take over Athens.

336 BCE
Alexander the Great
Alexander becomes king of Macedonia in northeastern Greece. He takes over surrounding regions, starting with Egypt.

86 BCE
Romans Invade
Soldiers from Rome, in what is now Italy, take over Athens. Rome rules Greece for nearly 300 years.

Many aspects of life in these poleis have shaped cultures across Europe and the Americas today. Ancient Athens has been a particularly strong influence. In the 6th century BCE, **democracy** was born in the city. Male **citizens** voted on laws and leaders. Modern science, **philosophy**, and building design all include ideas developed in ancient Greece, too. As a result, Greek history is present not only in its ruins and artifacts, but also in the living, modern-day culture.

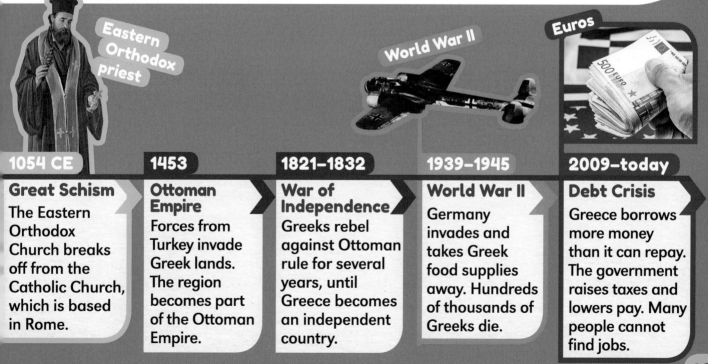

Eastern Orthodox priest

World War II

Euros

1054 CE
Great Schism
The Eastern Orthodox Church breaks off from the Catholic Church, which is based in Rome.

1453
Ottoman Empire
Forces from Turkey invade Greek lands. The region becomes part of the Ottoman Empire.

1821–1832
War of Independence
Greeks rebel against Ottoman rule for several years, until Greece becomes an independent country.

1939–1945
World War II
Germany invades and takes Greek food supplies away. Hundreds of thousands of Greeks die.

2009–today
Debt Crisis
Greece borrows more money than it can repay. The government raises taxes and lowers pay. Many people cannot find jobs.

It Came From Greece

White House

We have made inventions big and small! Ancient Greeks determined how big Earth is, and found out that it orbits the sun. We also made maps of the stars. Architects created a style of building withs columns and triangular roof sections called pediments. It is still used, including for the White House in Washington, D.C.! Our alphabet was developed some 3,400 years ago. It was based on another alphabet invented in Phoenicia to the east. Our alphabet is the basis of most modern writing systems, including the letters you are reading right now.

Before about 400 BCE, Greeks believed illness was a punishment from the gods. Hippocrates had a medical school on the island of Cos. He and other doctors there found that illness is caused by disease, not a god. Hippocrates wrote an oath, or promise, that doctors had to help people. It still guides doctors around the world today!

Ancient Greeks invented the Western theater we know today. Theaters were sometimes built into the sides of hills. Each row of seats was a little higher than the one before it, and everyone had a good view of the stage. Theaters were also designed so sound traveled well. Even someone sitting at the back could hear. In ancient Greece, men played all the parts and often wore masks. Smiling masks were used for comedies. Sad masks were for tragedies. Plays even had special effects. Actors playing gods sometimes "flew" using ropes. Pebbles on a thin sheet of metal could make the sound of rain.

Ancient Athens was the home of early public libraries. They held scrolls, not books with pages and covers. Early scrolls were long, handwritten rolls of paper made from a plant called papyrus. The scrolls were unrolled and read from one side to the other, not top to bottom. Some individual Greeks had their own private libraries. Schools did as well. The government ran larger public libraries.

Celebrate!

People follow a shrine called the Epitaphios through Kythnos on the Friday night before Easter.

Everyone loves a holiday. Yiorgos's favorite is Easter. Easter is the biggest holiday of the year in the Greek Orthodox religion. (About 98 percent of Greeks are Greek Orthodox.) Our family visits our mother's parents on the island of Kythnos. The holiday starts the Friday before Easter. Everyone follows a **shrine** through the streets. On Saturday night, we go to church until midnight, when each person lights a neighbor's candle. At home afterward, we have a special soup made from the heart and other organs of a lamb. The rest of the meat is roasted for Easter Sunday supper. We also hard-boil eggs, then dye them bright red! Some of the eggs are baked into tsoureki, a sweet bread.

We also use our red eggs in a game called tsougrisma. We take turns smacking the end of our egg against someone else's egg. If your egg doesn't crack, you hit the next person's egg. When one end breaks, you switch ends and keep going. The last person with an uncracked end will have a lucky year!

Gynaikokratia

January

Men and women trade traditional roles in northern Greece. Men do housework. Women visit friends and drink coffee. Everyone has a party together in the evening.

Carnival

February / March

About six weeks before Easter, we celebrate Carnival. The parade in Skyros is known for costumes of goat masks and skins! Patras has the biggest festival, with parades, balls, and even a treasure hunt.

Independence Day

March 25

This day celebrates the day in 1821 when our fight for independence officially started. There are parades and feasts.

Ochi Day ("No!" Day)

October 28

During World War II, Italy asked to move its army into Greece, but Greece said no. Now each year, we have military parades to celebrate our answer!

Make Red Eggs!

Ask an adult for help!

What you'll need:
Skins from 8 yellow onions, 1 tablespoon white vinegar, 2 ¼ cups water, 6 eggs, paper towel, olive oil

1 Make the dye: Put the onion skins, vinegar, and water in a pot. Once the water boils, cover the pot and reduce the heat. Cook 30 more minutes.

2 Let the dye cool. Then pour it through a strainer into a bowl to remove the onion skins.

3 Place the eggs in a medium-sized stainless steel pot. Pour the dye over the eggs to cover them. Bring it to a boil, and then lower the heat.

4 Stop cooking when the eggs are red or after 20 minutes!*

5 Cool, then rub the eggs with a paper towel and olive oil until they shine!

Tsougrisma

*If you want the eggs to be redder, let the pot cool after cooking, then put it in the fridge. Check the color every hour.

23

Football

Ancient Olympics

Time to Play

We Greeks love soccer. Like others in Europe, though, we call it football! It's our national sport. Yiorgos and I play with friends in the park, and we always support our country's team. I also like to play volleyball. Yiorgos prefers basketball. Greece's basketball team is among the best in Europe!

Of course, Greece has a long history of sports. Ancient Greeks invented the Olympics to honor Zeus, the king of gods. For nearly 1,200 years, the games were held every four years. Men ran footraces, boxed, and wrestled. They also threw a javelin, which is similar to a spear, and a flat disc called a discus.

Modern Olympics open with a series of runners carrying a flaming torch from Greece to the site of the games.

Tavli

The modern Olympics started in 1896. Countries from around the world still compete in these games every two years. Greece hosted the 2004 games in Athens and won 16 medals there.

We're not only into sports. We like to play games, too! A lot of Greeks play an ancient board game called *tavli* that the Egyptians invented. It looks a little like backgammon. Yiorgos is thoughtful when he plays, but I get excited and shout! Our dad also taught us games from when he was a kid, such as apples and *abariza*. Apples is a lot like dodgeball. Abariza is similar to tag, but with teams.

You Won't Believe This!

If two people say the same thing at the same time, Greeks believe they will get into an argument. But they can be saved from fighting by touching something red right away!

For thousands of years, people have been afraid of the Evil Eye. This is a glare from someone that can make bad things happen to you. Today, a lot of Greeks are still careful about the Evil Eye. They may not be sure it's real, but they protect against it just in case. Carrying something bright blue can help. Greek rooftops are often painted blue for this reason. Other people wear a symbolic blue eye (pictured) for protection. You can also spit three times after saying something nice to someone. This is meant to keep the Evil Eye from hurting that person. Our grandma always has a piece of garlic in her pocket as her defense.

Since ancient times, Greeks have been skilled sailors. Today, Greece has the largest number of commercial ships in the world! Commercial ships are any ships that carry goods or passengers for money.

We say *ne* for "yes" and *ochi* for "no." We also don't nod and shake our heads like Americans do. To show "no," we nod our heads up a little. To show "yes," we make a nodding downward movement with our heads.

Yes!
Ne!
No!
Ochi!

In Greece, we never leave the last bite of food or the last drop of our drinks behind. Many believe that if we do, all our secrets will be revealed!

27

Guessing Game!

Here are some other great sites around Greece. If you have time, try to see them all!

A

Twenty million years ago, these forests on an island in the Aegean Sea were covered by volcanic ash and preserved.

B

People from around the world come to these cliffs to rock climb.

1 Olympia

2 Kalymnos sea cliffs

3 Nisyros craters

4 National Marine Park of Alonissos and Northern Sporades

5 Meteora monasteries

6 Lesvos petrified forests

7 The Old Town of Rhodes

Visitors can step back in time in this town on the island of Rhodes. The town is surrounded by ancient stone walls.

E

F

This collection of six cliff-top monasteries, where monks and nuns live and worship, are found in central Greece.

This is the site of the original Olympic Games. In 67 CE, the Roman emperor Nero took part in the chariot race here. He had 10 horses, while other racers had only four. He fell off his chariot but was still awarded first place.

C

D

This spot in the Dodecanese Islands is famous for its **dormant** volcano. Craters steam, hiss, and bubble.

By the shore of Alonissos, snorkel or take a boat to see some of the incredible animals that live in this park.

G

Answer Key

1C, 2B, 3D, 4G, 5F, 6A, 7E

Preparing for Your Visit

You might have the chance to see Greece in person someday. Here are some tips that could help you prepare for a trip.

1 The currency in Greece is the euro. There are ATMs in many places, and visitors can withdraw euros from them. On some small islands, however, ATMs can be out of service for a few days at a time.

2 The climate varies between the mountains, which are generally cooler and are snowy in winter, and the sea-level areas, which have warmer weather. If you plan to visit, make sure you check the weather before packing!

3 There aren't many public bathrooms in Greece. A tourist's best bet is to pop into a café. Buy a little something from the café if you use their facilities. Also, the plumbing here isn't set up for paper. Expect to put used toilet paper in the trash container *next* to the toilet. And though most bathrooms have toilets, some may have a hole in the floor with spots for your feet on either side. Just squat down over the hole.

4 When visiting a church, keep your shoulders and knees covered. Visitors cannot take photographs with a flash inside churches—and never photograph a church's altar.

5 In a health emergency, 112 is the number to call. It is possible to speak to someone in English, 24 hours a day. The Tourist Police can help with large or small problems. Their number is 171. If you need an ambulance, dial 166.

The United States Compared to Greece

	United States of America (USA)	Hellenic Republic
Official Name	United States of America (USA)	Hellenic Republic
Official Language	No official language, though English is most commonly used	Greek
Population	325 million	Nearly 11 million
Common Words	yes, **no**, please, **thank you**	ne (NEH), **ochi (OH-hee)**, parakalo (pah-rah-kah-LOH), **efharisto (ef-hah-ree-STOH)**
Flag		
Money	**Dollar**	Euro
Location	North America	Southern Europe
Highest Point	Denali (Mount McKinley)	Mount Olympus
Lowest Point	Death Valley	Mediterranean Sea coast
National Anthem	"The Star-Spangled Banner"	"Ýmnos is tin Eleftherían"

So now you know some important and fascinating things about our country, Greece. We hope to see you someday touring an  ancient temple, snorkeling in the Mediterranean Sea, or enjoying a fun game of tavli. Until then . . . *andio* (ahn-DEE-oh). Good-bye.

Glossary

citizens
(SIT-i-zuhnz)
people who have full rights
in a particular country

civilization
(siv-uh-lih-ZAY-shuhn)
a developed and organized
society

democracy
(di-MAH-kruh-see)
a form of government in
which the people choose
their leaders in elections

dormant
(DOR-muhnt)
describing a volcano that
is currently not active, but
may be active again

murals
(MYOOR-uhlz)
large paintings done
on walls

myths
(MITHS)
old stories that express the
beliefs or history of a group
of people, or explain some
natural event

peninsula
(puh-NIN-suh-luh)
a piece of land that sticks
out from a larger landmass
and is almost completely
surrounded by water

philosophy
(fuh-LAH-suh-fee)
the study of truth, wisdom,
the nature of reality, and
knowledge

shrine
(SHRINE)
a building or small
structure that contains
objects associated with
a holy person

snorkeling
(SNOR-kuhl-ing)
swimming underwater
with a long tube that is
held in the mouth and
used to breathe

Index

Facts for Now

Visit this Scholastic website for more information on Greece and to download the Teaching Guide for this series:

www.factsfornow.scholastic.com   Enter the keyword **Greece**

About the Author

Anna T. Tabachnik is a Paris-based art director and designer, editor and author, traveler and rock climber.

Greece first captured her imagination in fifth grade when Mrs. Kjellgren read Greek myths to the class.